How Cars Changed the World

LEVEL 8
/y/

Teaching Tips

Purple Level 8

This book focuses on the grapheme /y/.

Before Reading
- Discuss the title. Ask readers what they think the book will be about. Have them support their answer.
- Discuss the book's focused grapheme: /y/. Explain that it can have four different sounds: /y/, long /e/, long /i/, and short /i/. Give examples of each, such as *yellow*, *happy*, *shy*, and *rhythm*.

Read the Book
- Encourage readers to read independently, either aloud or silently to themselves.
- Prompt readers to break down unfamiliar words into units of sound and string the sounds together to form the words. Then, ask them to look for context clues to see if they can figure out what these words mean. Discuss new vocabulary to confirm meaning.
- Urge readers to point out when the focused phonics grapheme appears in the text. What sound is it making?

After Reading
- Ask readers comprehension questions about the book. How have cars changed how we live? What other inventions have changed how we live?
- Encourage readers to think of words with the /y/ grapheme. On a separate sheet of paper, have them write the words. Group them by the different /y/ sounds.

© 2024 Booklife Publishing
This edition is published by arrangement with Booklife Publishing.

North American adaptations © 2024 Jump!
5357 Penn Avenue South
Minneapolis, MN 55419
www.jumplibrary.com

Decodables by Jump! are published by Jump! Library.
All rights reserved. No part of this book may be reproduced in any form without written permission from the publisher.

Library of Congress Cataloging-in-Publication Data is available at www.loc.gov or upon request from the publisher.

ISBN: 979-8-88524-781-8 (hardcover)
ISBN: 979-8-88524-782-5 (paperback)
ISBN: 979-8-88524-783-2 (ebook)

Photo Credits

Images are courtesy of Shutterstock.com. With thanks to iStockphoto. Cover – Shutterstock. p4–5 – Gorodenkoff, Fauzan Fitria. p6–7 – amnat30, Ion Mes. p8–9 – buzbuzzer, moreimages. p10–11 – dean bertoncelj, huyangshu. p12–13 – IN Dancing Light, vladimir salman. p14–15 – Artens, JULYP30. p16 – Shutterstock.

Which of these words rhyme?

Coffee

Fly

Berry

Sky

Very

Why do we invent new things? We invent new things to fix problems! When something new fixes a big problem, it can change the world.

What can you think of that has really changed the world?

When cars were invented, they made the world feel smaller and connected people more than ever. Understanding the things we invent can help us understand the world around us a little better.

We have come a long way from the animal-drawn carts of our ancestors. The car has changed how we travel and made travel much easier than it was.

Way back about 200 years ago, if you wanted to travel a long way for a nice day out, the trip could take up to 12 hours on a horse and cart!

When cars were first introduced in America, most were powered by steam and electricity instead of by gas. But soon, gas became the main fuel used to power cars.

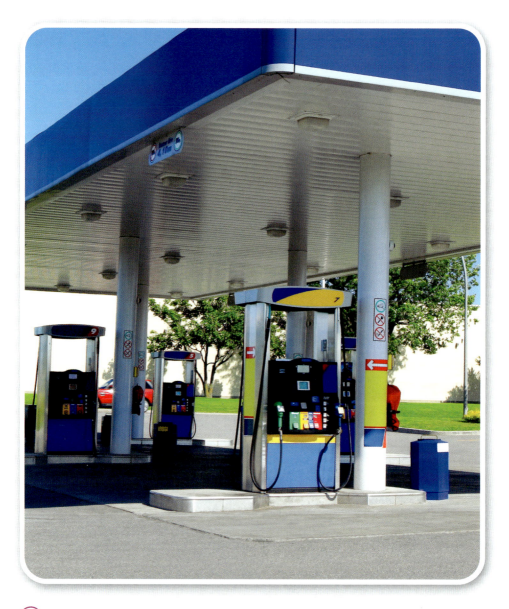

Even if early electric cars were popular, there was a big problem with them. Few towns or cities had electricity at this time.

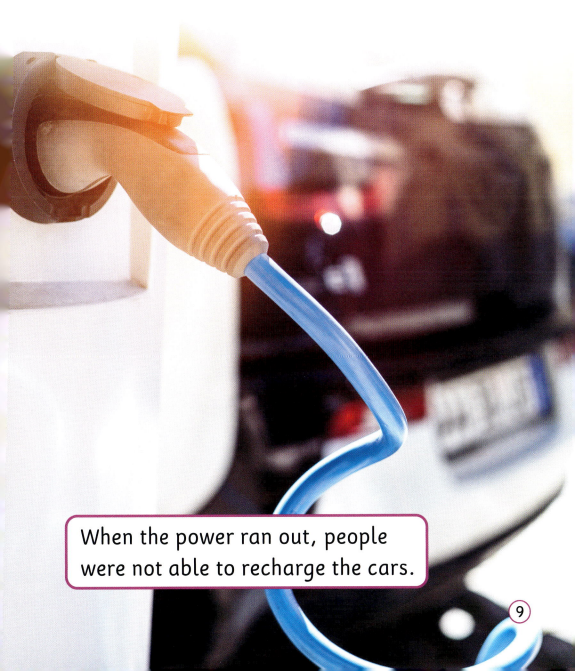

When the power ran out, people were not able to recharge the cars.

Henry Ford's gas-powered car, the Model T, put an end to cars powered by electricity. The Model T cost $650, while the electric roadster was a costly $1,750.

People didn't want to pay more than twice the price.

The success of the Model T led to an increase in the use of crude oil to make fuel for cars. Oil and gas became important, and more car companies started using it.

Oil rig

Henry Ford's Model T didn't just change which cars people got. Henry Ford changed the way people made cars with the very clever way the company made cars.

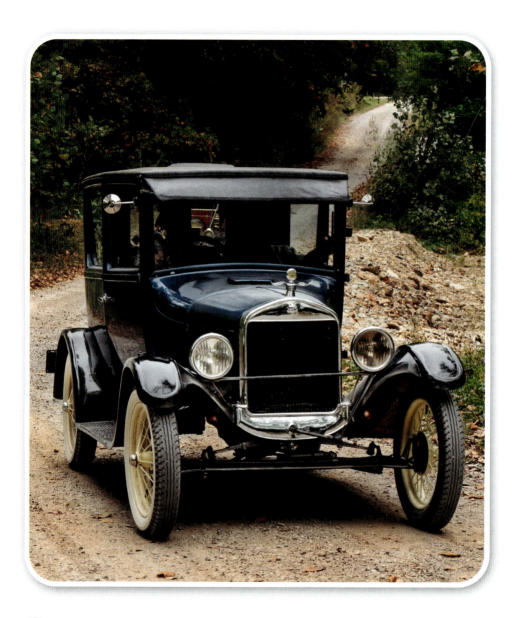

This was a method of making cars where instead of the engineers moving all their tools from one car to another, the cars carefully moved along a belt to the engineers.

Cars changed a lot about how we do things. People could travel farther and faster than they did in the past. People could have homes farther from where they worked and travel by car.

Every city and town has been made and remade with the car in mind. Roads have been cut into landscapes that stood unchanged for thousands of years.

Cars have had a very big impact on the world.

Say the name of each object below. Is the "y" in each a long /e/ sound or a long /i/ sound?

baby

bunny

spy

dry